THE ECONOMIC GUERRILLA

A GOLDEN OPPORTUNITY HANDBOOK

~

Mark T. Johnson

The Economic Guerrilla
A Golden Opportunity Handbook
by Mark T. Johnson

ISBN 0-87364-445-X
Printed in the United States of America

Published by Paladin Press, a division of
Paladin Enterprises, Inc., P.O. Box 1307,
Boulder, Colorado 80306, USA.
(303) 443-7250

Direct inquiries and/or orders to the above address.

Contents

Introduction

What is an Economic Guerrilla? He or she is a person who has developed attitudes and skills which provide a comfortable lifestyle during an economic crisis. What does this mean? This means that the Economic Guerrilla is capable of surviving extended periods of income loss without resorting to welfare, food banks, or crime. The Economic Guerrilla will generally reenter the mainstream economy more quickly than his counterparts. The Economic Guerrilla has resources available to effectively counter sudden income loss.

The training of an Economic Guerrilla, or EG, should start before the skills become necessary. This usually gives time for necessary attitudes and behavior to become second nature. An EG can learn the necessary fundamentals in the face of crisis quite successfully if he is prepared for a massive and rapid rethinking of his situation. Both of these methods will be addressed.

PART I
Good Times

Immediate Solutions

The person who is currently an active member of the mainstream economy is in the best position to start EG training. This person has a regular source of income and its associated comfort zone within which to work.

The first thing a person in this position should do is set up a few contingency plans. A good tool for planning is the "worst case scenario." You have just been laid off and your only source of income is unemployment payments. Can you survive without going into the red? Probably not, so the first thing we have to examine is debt load. With the exception of utility and possibly mortgage payments, every other debt you have now probably could have been avoided. From this point on, the EG will avoid future debts. How? Right now take all of your credit cards, every one of them, and burn them. Hard, isn't it? You have just eliminated one of the largest sources of your debt load. It can't get any bigger from this point. It can only get smaller until it no longer exists.

Let's stop for a moment. You may be thinking, "This guy is crazy if he thinks I'm going to burn my credit cards. That's the only way I can make it every month." If that's what you're thinking, you have just run into the first obstacle an EG has to overcome: attitude -- in this case shown by misplaced values.

Misuse of credit is the biggest trap of the so-called "consumer society." The average consumer has been conned by the advertising industry into thinking that he can have everything he wants now and pay for it a little at a time . . . later. Some of us delude ourselves into thinking that if we buy that little goody now, we can pay for it at the end of the month. Some people even get a certain amount of gratification from flashing a wallet full of plastic in front of others as if it is some type of status symbol. How many times have you engaged in this game of credit-card one-upmanship to see who can display the most prestigious credit card?

Oh, I know you never plan to use them, you like to have them just in case, right?

Credit issuers are no dummies. They know human nature and buying habits inside and out. That's why they're getting richer by the minute. They have teamed up with the advertising industry to convince you that you can have everything in the consumer world right now. They actually try to make you feel guilty if you don't use credit. Have you ever made a purchase and been asked, "Will that be on your account today?" What they are actually saying is, "You *are* worthy enough to have a card, aren't you?" Talk about intimidation and manipulation.

The EG is prepared to break out of this expensive

game by destroying his credit cards, paying off his accounts, and buying *only* when he can afford to pay cash. These are not easy things to do because they require a certain amount of self-discipline and sacrifice. Doing without some of the so-called necessities of life can even bring about a certain degree of social stigma. The thing to remember is that your critics are not going to pay your bills. Soon most of what you have will be paid for, and *they* will still be in debt. The idea behind being an EG is to travel light.

You've broken out of the credit-card trap; now what do you do? Well, even though your debt load is no longer increasing, it still has to be serviced. Why not service it as cheaply as possible? Talk to your bank about acquiring a debt-consolidation loan. In fact, shop around at several banks. The point of this exercise is to avoid paying credit-card interest rates from which the credit issuers make their money. When the bank reschedules your debt, two positive things happen: one, your charge accounts are paid in full, and two, you are paying a lower interest rate.

There is a way of using credit cards that benefits the EG. This method will only work if it is followed religiously with no deviation, which will require a high degree of self-discipline. This method involves knowing the billing dates of your creditors. If you are prepared to make your credit purchases and pay for them prior to the billing dates, then you have used your creditor's money for as long as a month and a half interest-free, while at the same time your money has been sitting in the bank collecting interest. This is a variation of the cash-only method that allows you to actually make money in the process. Once again, this is recommended only to those who are prepared to follow it strictly.

Now you have paid off the charge accounts and rescheduled your debts at lower interest rates. Where do you go from here? Take a look at your cash flow. Every household has certain fixed costs. These costs are your rent or mortgage payments, utilities, insurance, medical plans, groceries, automotive costs, clothing, and so on. Work out a budget to see what these costs are each month. The difference between your fixed expenses and income is that wonderful thing known as "disposable income." Here we come up against another example of wrong attitude. The very concept of disposable income can get you in trouble. The term implies that it is something to be disposed of, thrown away. How does one dispose of money? He spends it. See the subtle manipulation?

The EG doesn't have disposable income. He has *economic resources.* Economic resources are funds which the EG uses to provide for contingencies as well as lifestyle enhancement. How is this done? One of the oldest and most successful methods is the 10 percent method. Every pay period, allocate 10 percent of your net pay to a contingency fund. This should be a vehicle that does not allow you to have easy access like a savings or checking account. It also should not be overly difficult to access. A good accessibility would be one that requires thirty-day notice. Why thirty days? This will prevent impulse spending. You will have time to debate the merits of an expenditure. A contingency vehicle should provide you with higher than bank interest and should have allocations automatically deducted from your bank account. This will allow you to treat it as simply another bill, yet you will be actually paying yourself. Finally, it should also be a vehicle which will allow you a tax advantage. Many vehicles fit these categories and the EG would be well advised to spend some time with a reputable financial planner to examine which ones are best suited to his needs.

This type of savings, while not showing large growth at first, will really benefit the EG after the third or fourth year through the effects of compounded interest and regular contributions. The contingency vehicle will provide a cash-flow reserve to use in the event of crisis. To further enhance this vehicle, when your debt load is paid, some of those funds could also be diverted into the contingency vehicle.

Now that you have dealt with your debt load and have established a contingency reserve, how do you deal with the remainder of your economic resources? This is called your cash-on-hand. Most people will find that this figure will probably be quite small. In fact, this is where you may feel the effects of credit-card withdrawal the most. You may have even discovered that you are working for your creditors and not yourself. It's a good thing that you have come to grips with reality now rather than when you are in the middle of unemployment. There is one guaranteed method of increasing cash-on-hand.

Reexamine your budget and see if you can modify your lifestyle a bit. Isn't a postage stamp cheaper than a long-distance call? A letter is a lot more personal. Isn't brown-bagging cheaper than restaurant lunches?

Can you really afford those trendy convenience foods? Spend some time working out inexpensive yet nutritious meal planning and go shopping with a list instead of just an "idea." Do you really need to take the car this trip? Walking is cheaper than gasoline. What about personal habits? Do you smoke or drink? Figure out the costs. Are lights left on in vacant rooms? What about the thermostat? Dressing a bit warmer or maybe exercising a bit is cheaper than a utility bill. Have you been to your library lately? The library is the best single source of information on inexpensive ways of doing anything you can imagine, and it's free. Reading library books is also great free entertainment that enriches the individual, which is more than can be said for going to a club or watching television. Pets are wonderful, but can you really afford to feed and take care of one? Veterinarians aren't inexpensive. Do you really need that pair of designer jeans? Wouldn't a good six-dollar haircut be better than a thirty-dollar stylist treatment? I'm sure by now you've gotten the message about your budget. A good goal for an EG would be to have five hundred dollars cash-on-hand in the bank at all times. Once that has been achieved, try to double it. The extra five hundred dollars then gets diverted to contingency. Then try to double the five hundred dollars again.

Now we control our finances instead of them controlling us. Is that it? Not by a long shot. The EG now has to "sniff the wind." That means to know yourself first, and then know what is going on around you. The EG must be continually involved in self-analysis. You have to work very hard to understand exactly who and what you are. As much as possible, EGs should be aware of *why* they say what they say and do the things they do. This continual process of self-discovery will help in developing thought patterns and habits which will enhance the EG's lifestyle.

The EG armed with self-knowledge has to discover how that knowledge can be best utilized for self-enhancement. For the majority of people this means finding suitable employment. The EG who is currently employed is at a distinct advantage over the currently unemployed. The EG will spend time researching the field he wishes to enter. This means finding out what skills are required, what salaries can be expected, what the long-term employment prospects are, who are the local employers in that field, and who are the key people. A lot of this kind of information, once again, is at your library free of charge.

If skills are required, the EG will avail himself of adult education courses available to acquire the skills necessary. The EG will also develop contacts who may help him keep abreast of openings in the field he is pursuing.

The EG who is in a comfortable work environment will continually upgrade his skill levels through adult education or on-the-job training to increase his worth to the employer and establish job security. It is incumbent on the EG to follow the developments of his industry as a whole to enable him to have not only the skills demanded today, but those of the future as well.

The world of corporate politics is something with which the EG must be prepared to deal. The EG should be aware of those around him who are the actual power brokers within a company. The EG should try to act as a listening post on the grapevine while at the same time inputting nothing at all. The ability to listen and keep a confidence will serve the EG immeasurably. The EG should avoid expressing opinions at work. He should instead practice hearing the other person out and acknowledging the other's point of view while expressing neither agreement or disagreement. If at all possible, the EG should never mention anything about his nonwork activities. Above all else, the EG should never say anything to anybody that he would feel uncomfortable having the head of the company hear. Company politics is a fact of life and the EG would be best advised to maintain a neutral posture. If presented with a highly political environment, the EG may wish to keep a diary of various encounters and the nature of each. He may also wish to keep a log of daily activities to settle any disputes that may arise. Any journal of this type should be kept extremely confidential. It may be quoted from when needed.

Philosophy

You have just been given some very powerful tools for your economic arsenal. If you stop reading right now and think about what you have read, you'll probably agree that what I have said is possible and makes sense. You know what else will happen? *Nothing.* Why? You're still carrying around a lot of mental baggage which will sabotage any effort to become an EG. It has taken you a lifetime to develop your current lifestyle and financial habits (good and bad). It is going to take time to develop new ones.

Let's start with the basics. Why did you buy this book? To get an inside track? To make a lot of money without working hard? To find a "quick fix" or "Band-Aid" solution to financial crisis? To beat the system? If any of these reasons sounds familiar, you've got a problem. Let's get one thing straight right now.

There's no such thing as a free lunch.
You don't get something for nothing.

I really hope you believe that. If you don't accept that fundamental principle you may as well throw this book away, because it won't do any good whatsoever.

Many people believe that they really have very little control over their lives. They believe that life consists of random events which must be dealt with as best one can. People who subscribe to this school of thought find many reasons for lack of happiness and achievement. They point to the economy, the political system, the educational system, the multinational corporations, the Third World, the threat of nuclear war. All of these and more, such people believe, are responsible for the failure of many individuals to achieve their fullest potential. If you truly believe this, you'll never be an EG. Why? To believe any of the above is to externalize the responsibility for oneself. The EG must consciously and subconsciously believe that he is totally responsible for his own life. The EG eagerly acts to control the events in his life. The EG sacrifices to no one and expects no one to sacrifice to him.

The EG is not responsible for the state of the world and the world is not responsible for him. The EG relies upon his own powers of observation and analysis to arrive at truth. He refuses to act in accordance with the consensus if the consensus contradicts rational analysis. The EG acts in accordance with reality, i.e., that which is. The EG realizes that truth is reality and reality is truth. Internal conflict is inversely proportional to the degree of behavior consistent with reality. The higher the consistency, the lower the internal conflict.

The EG is constantly engaged in not the understanding of others, but of himself. The better an EG can understand his own actions, thoughts, and emotions, the better he can understand those around him. Self-knowledge generates inner strength which can never be subordinated to another. The EG is never dependent upon others for motivation and courage. These are constantly generated internally.

You may be thinking that you'll never have what it takes to be this type of person. You know something? You're absolutely right. On the other hand, you may be thinking that this type of person reflects your own values. You know something? You're absolutely right. Nobody can give you a magic formula for character. Not me, not your parents, not your teachers . . . nobody. You have to give it to yourself all alone.

I didn't intend for this section to be a full dissertation on philosophy. I primarily designed it to touch base with some concepts which I hope are already familiar to you. I would suggest reading Ayn Rand's, *For The New Intellectual*, for an expanded presentation of rational concepts. These philosophical foundations are necessary for the next step in becoming an EG.

Attitudes

Everyone wants to be liked. To that end, we constantly reflect morals and values which bring positive reinforcement from those around us. The group, however it's defined (family, friends, fellow employees, church), exerts a powerful influence on almost every aspect of our daily lives. This influence can be both beneficial and lethal to the EG. If the EG falls into the trap of externalizing his self-image (I truly believe I am who "they" say I am), his most valuable survival tool is lost. Let's examine some of these pitfalls.

GUILT

Guilt is perhaps the single most deadly enemy of the EG. In the hands of a skillful manipulator, it can completely stifle an individual. Guilt is used to belittle and render insignificant an act or thought. It is also used to place an individual in a state of repentance, in which he seeks the forgiveness of others. As long as forgiveness is withheld, the self-image is in a negative state. No progress can be made.

Guilt is most often felt when one fails to meet someone else's expectations. What this means in many cases is that you have failed to promote the self-interests of another. That other person, seeing his goals thwarted, will immediately use guilt to motivate you. Since you seek the approval of others, you will repent and give this person what he wants: positive reinforcement of his self-image. What you have gained is the destruction of yours.

Self-analysis is the strongest weapon against guilt. The EG is constantly engaged in it. He is continually examining why he thinks and acts the way he does in any given situation. This analysis produces an internally generated and constantly improving self-image. If an act is wrong, the EG will examine the reason it is wrong using rationality and will, it is hoped, adjust his behavior accordingly. If an action is right, it will receive the same scrutiny. This will produce a personal moral code which reflects the rational self-interests of the EG. It is this code and this code alone that the EG uses to judge his actions. A briefer way of saying this is that the EG needs a strong sense of self-responsibility.

The human species does not always act in a rational manner. The EG will find himself many times acting irrationally, even after fully contemplating an action or thought and recognizing its irrationality. The important difference here is that the EG will examine the true motives behind these irrational acts and discover more about himself. This is an extremely powerful tool for the EG because it is a door to the subconscious mind. It is at this level that real change must take place.

Most people find that they can accept a rational premise on an intellectual, conscious level but will act in contradiction to it. When this happens they usually ask *why*. It may help to know that when the conscious and subconscious mind are in contradiction, the will of the subconscious mind will prevail in most cases. This is why it is so important to really think hard about why one acts irrationally at the time the action occurs. This is when the two parts of the mind are open to communication, and the effects of rational analysis can imprint the subconscious and become second nature. This is also when the conscious mind can explore the contents of the subconscious and influence what's there.

I strongly advise that when you start self-examination, you should be prepared to accept everything you find. It is a difficult process that will reveal both the very beautiful and the very ugly sides of yourself. Everyone has these things inside himself. When you start cataloging who you are, you will discover that you have a lot in common with both the loved and the despised in your life. What you want to happen is the insertion of positive, rational self-enhancement at the primary motivation level.

SELFLESSNESS

Selflessness is held up to us as a virtue to be obtained by all. It means to give freely and generously of oneself to any who may demand it with no expectation of reward or recompense. Sounds beautiful, doesn't it?

It is deadly, repeat *deadly!*

Selflessness, by all of its various names (charity, sense of humanity, generosity, caring, etc.), is usually most loudly praised by those who want something. What they want is the fruit of your effort upon which they place a high value. What they offer in exchange is freedom from your guilt (which they impose) and their approval and forgiveness (on which they hope you place a high value). This is external manipulation of the self-image at its worst.

The promoters of selflessness attempt to make you feel ashamed of your success. They will try to convince you either blatantly or subtly that your success is only the result of luck and chance or worse, the result of the exploitation of others. They will attempt to convince you that wealth and material possessions which enhance your personal lifestyle are somehow *evil.* They want you to purge yourself of these evil things by giving the things away -- a donation usually given to those who are trying to convince you. After your donations, a magical thing happens! The evil money and possessions you worked for and earned suddenly become *blessed* when given *selflessly* to these guilt-mongers. To make matters worse, the guilt-mongers generally lie in wait while you earn more evil wealth so they can strike again.

The concept of helping others is one of the most beautiful characteristics of being human. I do not oppose it at all. However, I suggest that helping others be based on rationality instead of pity.

Take a good look at potential recipients of your help. These recipients should be doing everything within their capabilities to improve their own situation. They should not be waiting for help because they "deserve" it. Ask yourself how you can best serve the recipient. If the answer is cash, stop right there! Cash in itself is never an answer. It will only cause potential problems.

To give someone cash is to impose an obligation to repay, which is an unnecessary guilt trip. It also makes the recipient answerable to you as to how the cash is spent. This is involuntary servitude which you have no right to expect. It will cause bad feelings if for some reason the cash is not repaid. Cash, while perhaps providing temporary relief from economic crisis, does not address the real problem areas of personal management. The most useful assistance you can give another is to show him how he can improve his lot through his own efforts.

Showing someone different perspectives accomplishes many positive things. It will cause him to think more effectively. It will work only if he uses it so there is no indebtedness. The recipient still maintains complete control and responsibility for his life. Your cash flow is not reduced. The recipient will have greater respect for you in the long run.

If the EG decides to give something away, it should be just that, a gift. Do not expect gratitude, thanks, appreciation, or help if you need it. Let's look at the reasons. Pride is a powerful force in most of us. We will do any number of things to maintain it and its companion, self-respect. The act of going "hat-in-hand" to someone and asking for help is demeaning. What we are saying in effect is, "I have failed to accomplish this task. I need your help because my resources are inadequate." This is not a comfortable position to be in. The recipient is standing "naked" before a donor and admitting failure and defeat. Ironically the only possible "winner" in this scenario is the recipient, not the donor.

If the recipient gets aid, two things happen. First, the recipient is grateful for immediate assistance. Second, the recipient immediately begins to resent the donor. Why? The donor has seen the recipient naked and stripped of pride and for the rest of the recipient's life, the recipient will know someone has seen him as such. This resentment usually manifests itself in money not being repaid. The recipient rationalizes, "So-and-so can afford it, he isn't hurting." If the aid is repaid, the attitude is, "I finally got that so-and-so paid off." On the other hand, if the donor doesn't give in the first place, he's a selfish so-and-so. In any case, the donor winds up being maligned.

Let's look at the concept of "If you help others, they will help you later." The first thing to examine in this statement is who has to help first -- you. The assistance in return payment to you comes *later*. In examining that term *later*, I have found that the roles of donor and recipient are very rigidly defined in life. Contrary to popular belief, the roles seldom reverse. Both donor and recipient reflect attitudes that perpetuate their roles. Generally, donors remain donors and recipients remain recipients. What happens when the roles reverse? First, let's take a look at what happens to the donor who turns recipient.

The theory is that if we need help, the first ones we

should seek out are those whom we have helped. These people will be, supposedly, more than willing to repay the kindness that we have shown them in the past. *That ain't the way it goes*! If you go to someone whom you've helped in the past, this is the more likely scenario. The person you helped will first go into ego overload. He'll think to himself, "Well, well, well. Here is Mr. High-and-Mighty come down on his knees, begging me for help. Boy, am I going to enjoy this." He may not say this to your face, but you can bet your bottom dollar he's thinking it. Now one of two things will happen. The person to whom you are appealing will refuse to help you and let you know in no uncertain terms who is the donor and who is the recipient. If, on the other hand, he decides to help you, the terms will be exceptionally demeaning. In either case the goal is the same -- to reduce your self-respect as much as possible, i.e., "knock you off your high horse."

Sound a bit unfair? You bet it is! You are dealing with people who already have a rigid mind-set as far as donors are concerned. Donors are the fat cats, capitalists, opportunists, exploiters, lucky -- *the enemy*. Don't even try to confuse these people by presenting *facts*. You are dealing with *invincible ignorance*.

Let's assume that a recipient suddenly reaches donor status. The theory states that this person will gladly help those who were so kind as to help him when he was in need. Remember Gershwin's *Porgy and Bess*? "It ain't necessarily so!" This character has a very short memory. His attitude is, "I got mine, to heck with the rest of the world. Who helped me when I needed it?" This character is the main source of negative attitudes against the successful. He will flaunt his affluence and spit in the eye of anyone worse off than he. He will continually try to advance himself through the efforts of others and claim all the credit and glory for "his" achievements.

The EG is left with a dilemma. His sense of humanity urges him to help others. His sense of caution holds him back. Does a solution exist? You bet. Anonymity. If you are going to give something away, you should expect neither praise nor scorn. Do it anonymously. This can be applied to any type of help. If your desire to help is sincere (only you can answer that), there is no need for the recipient to know the source of help. Your ego doesn't require personal gratitude and the recipient doesn't need the additional burden of indebtedness.

SUCCESS AND WEALTH

Your attitude toward success and wealth will be the major determinant of your obtaining them. Old platitude? Yes, but with perhaps a different perspective. It is very possible that your attitude toward success and wealth has been affected by *failure practitioners*.

Failure practitioners preach a doctrine of mediocrity. They will tell you that to be successful is somehow wrong or evil. They will tell you that wealth is sinful. They wish to maintain the status quo by discouraging any attempt at excellence. This element will actively condemn or even thwart individuals who resist this doctrine. The failure practitioners will use many tactics such as guilt, ridicule, sabotage, intimidation, and ostracism.

Have you ever heard that poverty is a virtue? How about, "The meek shall inherit the earth"? What about there being nothing wrong with being poor? Remember hearing that the rich only think about themselves and not the rest of the world? High profits are really responsible for every misery in the world, right?

If any of the above sounds familiar or has validity in your life, the failure practitioners have had their effect. If nothing else, they have planted malicious seeds in your subconscious which could very well act to your detriment as an EG if you let them. Let's establish something right now. *Poverty sucks*! I have yet to meet any poor person who wouldn't jump at the chance to become suddenly rich. In fact, quite a number of rich people started out as poor people. Poverty is not honorable or enriching spiritually. Poverty is going without, and suffering. Poverty is hardship and pain. Poverty is not a goal to be obtained, it is something to escape from. Anyone who tells you that poverty is enriching and its burden morally uplifting is either deluding himself or benefiting from your misery.

There is nothing wrong with being rich as long as the wealth is obtained honestly. I cannot think of a situation where a person can honestly earn wealth without improving the lives of others. Henry Ford had the desire to become rich. He did it with the automobile. How many hundreds of thousands of people have benefited from his efforts? The factory workers who could buy houses and send their children to universities. The fellow who owns the garage down the street has something to repair. Engineers can design roads and freeways. Parking-lot attendants can pay the rent. Henry Ford has been dead for many years, yet the positive effects of his desire to become rich honestly still live on. I can find no fault with that. The same scenario applies whether the company is a multinational corporation or a mom-and-pop operation.

The United States of America presently enjoys the highest standard of living of any country on Earth. This standard of living is the direct result of people desiring to get rich and making it happen. These producers and contributors are those responsible for the state of health, wealth, and welfare in the world as we know it today. Our cars, homes, conveniences, technology, standard of health care, and the clothes we wear all stem from a desire to obtain wealth. The failure practitioners have contributed nothing except guilt and mediocrity.

Success is defined in many ways, but the way to obtain it is consistent hard work and persistence. To succeed in anything takes dedication, energy, blood, sweat, and tears. It never comes easy to anyone. That is why so many failures occur today. To obtain success in any endeavor is something of which you can be proud. You have succeeded where others have failed. There's nothing wrong with that. Human progress is measured in terms of success, not failure. Those who succeed get rewards while those who fail get condolences. I prefer rewards.

The "failure practitioners" are all around us. I am sorry to say that they seem to take a special delight in destroying potential EGs. The EG can expect scorn, ridicule, derision, resentment, and downright hostility from the failure practitioners. The reasons are a bit complex, but consistent with human nature. The EG is a glaring affront to failure practitioners. The EG represents everything failure practitioners aren't. The EG is self-confident, determined, self-reliant, ambitious, and goal-oriented; an achiever and a doer. Failure practitioners will use anything in their power to destroy an EG's will to succeed. They are failures in their own lives and very comfortable with their mediocrity and normalcy. They fit in with the consensus. The EG upsets the apple cart by showing them what can be accomplished with a little effort and ambition. Instead of emulating the EG, the failure practitioner will do what he does best -- attempt to induce failure.

How do you spot a failure practitioner? Like any other "professional," he uses jargon. Listen for it:

"What makes you think you're so hot?"

"Who do you think you are?"

"All you care about is yourself."

"Why should things be any different for you?"

"You can't change the way things are."

"Are you sure you know what you're doing?"

"You really think you're somebody special, don't you?"

"Nobody else thinks like you do."

"Nobody else controls their lives, why should you be different?"

"Why don't you give up this silly idea and get back to normal?"

The one common thread in the jargon of the failure practitioners is an attempt to instill doubt in one's abilities. Once there is an element of doubt, the majority of the failure practitioner's job is done. To accept doubt is to accept the failure practitioner as an authority figure. If the EG refuses to accept this authority, the next step is rejection and ridicule from the failure practitioner. If the EG returns to seek favor and acceptance he is no longer an EG. If he continues on his way, keeping his own counsel and using his own mind, he succeeds.

Does this seem a bit hard and cynical? It's intended to be. We are playing for the highest stakes: personal success. This is not something to be taken lightly because you don't get many chances to make it. An EG has to learn that not everyone shares his beliefs, and some will actually despise him for his, and will work to his disadvantage if he lets them.

Human Relationships

The field of human relationships is very wide and complex. What I'll present in this chapter are some concepts and guidelines which should assist the EG in maintaining positive, mutually beneficial relationships.

As far as we have been able to prove, the phenomena we call life exists only on Earth. Our powers of observation reveal no other form of life in the known universe. That means as humans we are all we have. We have to look out for each other. Each of us enjoys a life made possible by the efforts of others, both living and dead.

Each of us has the responsibility to improve upon what has gone before. The degree to which the individual succeeds is the degree to which all of mankind succeeds. This is a pretty hefty responsibility until you consider the alternative. The degree to which the individual fails is the degree to which mankind fails.

Each of our lives is intertwined and meshed to the lives of everyone else. Man is unique (not better, not worse) among living creatures in that he can choose how to interact with those around him. He can choose to interact positively or negatively in any situation. The rational self-interests of the EG are promoted if he endeavors to interact with everyone positively or at least, not negatively. Self-analysis will reveal to the EG that everyone he meets is a complete human being. We all have dreams, feelings, joys, sorrows, thoughts, ambitions, needs, and desires. He will grant at least the amount of respect to others that he expects for himself.

The EG will quickly discover that very few human interactions exist in which he cannot act positively. Unfortunately, this small number of situations will enter everyone's life. Even in this environment the EG will benefit if he treats his "opponent" with respect and dignity.

The EG will find that just about everyone responds positively to a kind word and a warm smile. While the EG should never subordinate himself to another, he should realize that others may be at least as capable as he in many areas. Most people wish to avoid conflict of any kind and will only act negatively if they feel threatened or attacked. The EG should be aware of this and attempt to maintain a nonthreatening environment which promotes progress.

All people are not created equal. They are created unique. The EG will learn to appreciate the uniqueness of each person, as well as the similarities. Judgments about people are difficult to make. The EG knows that he cannot judge any individual without living that person's life. He can, however, judge whether or not to continue a relationship. That judgment should be based on rational self-interest. Does the relationship represent a balanced, value-for-value exchange?

People are neither inherently evil nor inherently good. They simply are. The important thing is not to attempt to understand every human action, but to attempt to fully understand yourself and be prepared to spend a lifetime doing it. To the degree that you understand yourself, you will understand those around you.

Income

We have already taken steps to eliminate or reduce our debt load. We have established an economic contingency plan, we have trimmed our budget, and we cleared some cobwebs from our thought process. If you will remember, we don't have a lot of cash-on-hand, and that is the situation we wish to correct. Many of you will have just one income, and that leaves you economically vulnerable. Without that income, you're immediately placed in a crisis situation. The whole idea is to avoid that scenario.

For many of you, diversified income means either a part-time job or side venture. Let's deal with the part-time job first. The EG will quickly realize that part-time jobs are usually low paying and consume a large amount of energy, if pursued while working at a full-time career. This usually leaves one too physically and emotionally drained to do anything but work and sleep, which is not the best condition under which to live. You also wind up being dependent on the economic interests of not one, but two employers. This totally defeats the purpose behind becoming an EG, which is to exert the highest degree of control possible over one's economic circumstances.

The next steps will be hard for many people. Our formal education generally trains us to be employees. The employee mentality is instilled in us at a very early age and is reinforced almost continually throughout our lives. How many people do you know who are employees, and how many are self-employed? I'll bet that over 90 percent of the people you know are employees. There is absolutely nothing wrong with being an employee. However, let's examine your alternatives.

The marketplace is where the EG finds his security and future. What does this mean? Everyone has talents and abilities for which the marketplace is willing to pay. Employment is usually the transaction that we are most familiar with. We sell certain skills and abilities to an employer for a set amount of money. Most people stop marketing themselves at this point. This is the point where the EG begins.

Remember that, as it was mentioned earlier, the EG has to be involved in continual self-analysis and evaluation. This process will provide the EG with a constantly updated skill and talent inventory. It is this inventory that the EG utilizes and markets to the highest bidder. Marketing your skills requires a certain degree of expertise in self-promotion. It will also require some efficient time management if the EG is presently employed -- or even if he isn't.

Let's briefly examine self-employment before we discuss skill marketing. The EG must follow certain guidelines. The first and foremost is simple. *Keep your mouth shut!* Many would-be EGs ruin their chances by setting up a company and promptly bragging to all and sundry about the money that will come rolling in. In the case of the employee EG, it doesn't take too long before an employer feels that this person is more concerned with his own enterprises than the company's. Instant termination. Believe it or not, the average employer has no use for someone with the drives and ambitions of the EG. The employer prefers someone who will fit nicely into the corporate mold. Keep in mind our earlier discussion on corporate politics.

Your local public library has many books available that deal with setting up a small business either full-time or part-time. I will not waste a lot of time here by reinventing the wheel. The main thing that the EG should be concerned with is the cheapest way to structure a company that will serve the EG now and in the future. You don't need a lot of money and you don't need expensive lawyers. You will need to do research (once again, the resources at your public library are free), and you will need to spend time.

Now we are ready to look at what you are to market. What the EG is looking for is something that he controls as much as possible. Your product(s) should be an item or idea that result from your own efforts. You should try to stay away from things that pay you a commission or percentage. These types of products require a lot of effort on your part to market while the majority of the revenue goes to someone else. You should look for something that you can do entirely on your own with only the help of a spouse (if needed). Since this will probably start off as a part-time, marginally capitalized project, you will have neither the time nor the resources to support employees.

As a new business, you have to reach the largest possible market in the shortest possible time. This rule applies regardless of what you are marketing. This means advertising. No business can survive without advertising. I've heard many small and unsuccessful businessmen say, "I can't afford advertising." I say you can't afford *not* to advertise. Allow me to be the first to tell you that advertising isn't cheap. For a new business it may be the single largest budget item. The EG has to know how to get the most mileage from each advertising dollar.

Mail-order marketing has proven very successful for many EGs. Mail order supports a wide variety of products and services. Your advertisement reaches a large potential market and acts as a twenty-four-hours-a-day, seven-days-a-week salesman. Mail order doesn't require the overhead of a store-type operation such as rent, utilities, and display. Mail order doesn't require face-to-face contact so the EG isn't handicapped by race, gender, physical appearance, etc. Mail order can be operated from one's home.

Many mail-order marketing books are available for free at your public library, so I will leave it to you to read them. I will give some advice on advertising. Stick with a well-designed display ad placed in a monthly publication. Classified ads aren't nearly as visible as a display ad. Quality monthly magazines such as *Good Housekeeping*, *Popular Science*, or *Esquire* reach a large audience and are very seldom thrown away. If you place an ad in such a periodical, each copy in which your ad appears will probably be read by several people in addition to the original purchaser. These magazines usually wind up in libraries as well, which gives you even more exposure. Try to avoid having your ad appear in every issue unless by this means your sales are phenomenal. It is better to place your ad in every third issue at first to conserve your cash flow.

If you can't afford the national monthly magazines at first, then try for the weekly local newspapers. The ones with free circulation are best. They reach every home within a given area and your ad will last at least a week.

Whichever form of media you decide upon, research it first. Once again, your public library's business section has publications which carry the advertising rates and circulation figures of just about every publication in print. Read them.

I don't want to leave you with the impression that if you sell your widget through mail order, all you have to do is sit and watch money come in the mail slot. *It ain't that easy!* Mail order is like any other business. It succeeds only with hard work and smart decisions. You can quite easily lose your shirt. It is a means to market a product or idea that is very time efficient. Do your research first.

Obviously, mail-order marketing is not suited for every type of business. If, for example, you repaired small appliances at home, you would find mail-order marketing inappropriate. The same would apply if you were breeding animals or giving music lessons. Advertising will still be very necessary. The key thing, once again, is research. Go to your library and read about low-budget, effective advertising. Find out which methods will work best for your products or services.

Let's spend some time talking about starting capital. Every business requires capital to get started. The EG has to be prepared to invest capital in himself. How much money should you be prepared to spend? That depends on the type of business being considered. I will give one familiar piece of gambler's advice. Don't invest more than you are prepared to lose. The failure of all kinds of business is a very real fact of life; the EG is not immune to the effects of the market. As a very rough figure, I would suggest that a part-time venture be capitalized with at least five thousand to ten thousand dollars. Don't let those figures scare you. Many successful EGs started out with an awful lot less. I know of many who started with one hundred dollars. Those figures are mentioned to allow enough capital for the business to handle the unexpected (expect it regularly) without having to borrow from other income. The EG should be prepared to reinvest all revenues into the business for at least a year to allow it to grow and generate its own operating capital. Forget about borrowing starting capital. All you will be doing is incurring a debt load. Use the other principles I've outlined to accumulate capital. It's slower, but you won't be indebted to anyone if it doesn't work out.

There is one more trap to look out for: the "snake oil merchants." These guys usually travel from town to town holding "free seminars" in fancy hotels. They promise to show you how to "unlock your hidden talents" or "discover the real secrets of getting rich" and sometimes "how to make a million without risking one cent." These guys prey on two types of people. First they look for the person who believes in miracles. This is the type of person who is looking for someone to open a hole in the top of his head and pour in the "magic knowledge" for being successful, rich, and famous. The second type of person the snake oil merchants look for is the potential EG. This is a person who knows he has what it takes to do more than he is doing but needs someone or something to give him that "extra push." What the snake oil merchant is actually doing is trying to sell you yourself.

These guys usually have a course they are selling which usually costs around four hundred dollars for the first of a series. These courses are mainly motivational in nature. They don't reveal anything you haven't heard or don't already believe. They don't contain anything that you can't pick up at your library for free. Just ask your librarian for the books on personal motivation and positive thinking. The so-called "business seminars," ironically enough, usually mention the library as one of the main resources for a small business. They usually tell you this *after* they have your money.

One thing you have to remember when dealing with snake oil merchants is human nature. If you had a "surefire" way of making a million, would you tell everyone about it? Would you sell it for a lousy four hundred dollars? Does General Motors sell its corporate planning to Toyota? When people have a "good thing" going for themselves they don't spread it around. I am telling you about concepts that aren't particularly new or original. I am not telling you how I specifically apply them other than to say that I do apply them daily. I am not about to help my potential competition. What these guys are really doing is selling these courses by letting you think there is some kind of shortcut to success. Remember what I said a few pages ago? *There's no such thing as a free lunch. You don't get something for nothing.* Now we are ready to market ourselves . . . at last.

What to Sell?

Everybody has some skill or knowledge for which other people are willing to pay money. Let's pull out that personal inventory. What do you do particularly well? Are you a good cook? Are you good with children? Can you budget with limited resources? Are you a good woodworker? Are you a gardener? Are you technically inclined? Each of these talents is highly marketable.

A good cook can sell recipes and meal-planning ideas through mail order. Children's "rainy day" or "long drive" activities are very marketable, as are child-rearing skills, particularly problem-solving techniques. Home handyman plans are in demand, as are well-made domestic products, especially toys. A lot of people are interested in "green-thumb" secrets and techniques, especially when written for your particular climatic and soil region. Multitudes of the high-tech gizmos on the market break down and need to be repaired. The market is always looking for that perfect gadget. New applications for existing gadgets are constantly popping up. Money management skills are in high demand. Why not sell yours? Adult education is very popular. It seems that you can learn just about anything in night school. How about teaching others a skill you have? Take a proposal to your local school board.

As you can see, I've just scratched the surface. Once again your library can provide you with a lot of information on successful, at-home businesses. I can't tell you which one would be best for you. That is something you have to decide. Once again, you need to do the research. I can only give a few pointers. Whatever you decide upon, do it as well as you can. Imagine yourself as the customer. What would you expect? Give your customers the best value for their dollar. They expect and deserve it. Don't make commitments or claims on which you can't deliver. You will only get irate customers, and then no customers. Make the customer glad he did business with you instead of someone else.

It is possible to be professional while at the same time keeping an eye on costs. When considering purchasing anything for your business, ask yourself if you *really* need it. Is there a cheaper substitute? Can you make money with it? How soon? Can you borrow or rent it from someplace? Can you make it yourself? Think cheap. Thousands of people are eager to sell you "absolutely must haves" for your business. Let them sell to your competition.

The Hard Way

You may have noticed by now that I have left wide holes in this text. This is for a very good reason. This is *not* a "how-to" manual. I have no intention of spoon-feeding you everything you need to know. If you need that kind of support, you'll never be an Economic Guerrilla. The honest truth is that the drive and strength necessary to be an EG must come from inside you. I can't put it there, nor can anyone else. If you've got what it takes, you have 95 percent of what you'll need. Research will provide an additional 2 percent and experience another 2 percent. I expect this text to provide no more than 1 percent. You see, it is really up to *you*.

I could write an autobiography outlining my own experiences in detail, but it wouldn't serve as anything more than perhaps entertaining reading. Why? You're not me. You can't live my life, you have to live your own. The snake oil merchants will tell you if you follow their plans *exactly*, they will guarantee your success.

What they are not telling you is that it is impossible to follow someone else's (or even your own) philosophy 100 percent, and without error. I have given you some very basic guidelines which many of you will consider just plain common sense, and in many respects they are. The hard-and-fast "rules" will have to be made up as you go along. They will be *your* rules for *your* life. If you feel comfortable with the EG mind-set, the odds will be in your favor for maintaining a comfortable lifestyle.

PART II
Bad Times

Down and Dirty

O.K. You've read about how to avoid economic disaster. Unfortunately you bought this book just a bit too late. You're up to your ears in crisis, and you need help and need it fast. You're damn desperate and you don't know where to turn, because all the doors were closed a long time ago.

Just in case you have skipped the beginning of this manual and started reading at this point, I am going to give you a quick course in attitudes. The very first obstacle the Economic Guerrilla must conquer is himself. Right now, *you* are probably the biggest obstacle to your success. This is because you are still using attitudes and morals that worked quite well when you had a steady source of comfortable income. Let's get one thing straight right now. The Economic Guerrilla plays by an entirely different set of rules. To survive in your present situation you will have to pitch a lot of useless propaganda that has been clouding your brain. The Economic Guerrilla uses one rule as the basis for all of his actions. *You have the right to the opportunity to survive to the best of your ability.* That's it!

Think about what you have just read. The first thing that probably comes to mind is that you have a lot more rights than that. *Wrong!* All that any of us is ever given is an opportunity. It is completely in our control to use it or not use it. Again you say that many of the situations in life we cannot control. *Wrong!* If you use sober reflection and are totally honest with yourself, you will discover that in your adult life just about everything you have ever done or will ever do is in your total control -- including reading this sentence. All of our adult experiences are the results of choices that each of us makes every day. Even not making a choice is making a choice.

You are now going through economic hardship as a result of choices that you made. Think about that for a while. If you examine things carefully you will realize that your present difficulties are actually the results of decisions that you made. Isn't that a hell of a slap in the face? Here you are wondering where your next meal is coming from, with your back right against the wall, and I come along and tell you it's *your* responsibility. All you have to do is turn on the tube or read a paper to know that it's not your fault, right? It's the economy, the imports, the multinationals, the political climate, interest rates, all of that but definitely not your responsibility. *Wrong!* When things were going well and you had lots of money and the job looked great, whose responsibility was that? Didn't you rightfully take credit for your achievements? Weren't you justifiably proud of your standard of living? Perhaps you are a little angry now, but I think you see the point. You are totally responsible for yourself.

None of us can see into the future. You definitely did not decide to be without an income. You did decide to work for a particular employer, make a specific investment, or say a particular statement. In all likelihood, at that time you made what you thought was the right decision, or at least the best of all visible alternatives. In any event, there is nothing to be gained by getting uptight over yesterday. Cut it loose right now. The Economic Guerrilla realizes that the biggest brain-killer, besides wrong attitude, is getting hung up on yesterday's mistakes and not looking at today and tomorrow.

Let's get away from philosophy and take a look at reality. You are now in a state of either reduced or nonexistent income. You know damn well that the bills are going to keep on coming. You also know that you are going to get hungry pretty quickly. You are grabbing at straws trying to hold things together. You wish that I would hurry up and give you something that you can use to turn into cash, right now. I already have, but it probably flew right by you. Go back and read up to this part again. Maybe it will begin to sink in a bit. It takes a while, so don't get angry.

The first thing I am going to suggest that you do is very simple: Relax. Take a deep breath and just relax. It's not the end of the world. As a matter of fact, you may be in the strongest position you will ever be in. You have nothing to lose. There is nothing anybody can take away now. Don't let paranoia get to you. If it does, you are only going to waste precious energy and time worrying about things you shouldn't worry about. Take a look at the problem and its solutions, and do your best to keep going. I know you are probably saying that's easy for me to say. Listen buddy, I've been there. I've been so hung up on bills that I used to wake up in the morning with the dry heaves just because of worry and anxiety. I've tried to figure out how to feed several mouths with two dollars in my pocket, and this was before food banks. I know what it feels like to hear job interviewers lie through their teeth, telling you that they will "definitely" get in touch with you. I know the bitter taste of cold rejection that comes from sending countless resumes to box numbers. You don't have any monopoly on misery. You may have cornered the market on self-pity, though.

When I was very young, I went crying to my mother with the old lament, "Nobody likes me!" She comforted me for a while and then told me that if I was looking for pity, I could find it in the dictionary; it's listed under "p" and comes after "pathetic." She would give me love, help, and understanding, but no pity. I loved my mother for those words and I haven't been able to thank her enough.

Now back to you. The fact is that to survive you are going to have to reassess your entire lifestyle. You cannot escape that. You may have to move, lose your car, lose your credit rating, and a lot of the little luxuries you used to enjoy. Forget restaurants, movies, new clothes, booze, nightclubs, rock concerts, fancy entertaining, expensive gifts, records, and expensive hobbies. *You're broke!* You are going to have to trim a lot of deadwood from your life. You cannot afford the luxury of carrying it around. I can assure you that all of the places in which you won't be spending money will survive quite well -- and will not lift one finger to help you. Another fact to remember: Your survival is the most important reality. You are not in any position to be generous with your life skills. If you have no ready cash, liquidate some assets. Sentiment won't feed you, but cash will.

It is paramount that the Economic Guerrilla keep foremost in his mind that anything that is not contributing to his daily survival is deadwood and must be cut away. This applies regardless of whether it is plant, animal, mineral, or even human. This may very well be a painful task that may seem heartless and cold. However, survival is tough. You are in a state of war. You cannot afford to lose. You have to get rid of both yesterday's attitudes and yesterday's trappings. You have been disabled in the war and you have to lighten your load to make it in for repairs. You are making a down payment on tomorrow and in order to make it, you must travel light. The Economic Guerrilla is very nomadic in nature. Is all of this too high a price to ask? What price freedom?

Now let us explore actual survival strategies. I've taken a lot of time and many pages on attitudes and philosophy. The development of your economic-survival attitude is ten times more important than any tactic I can show you. If your attitude is right, you can make your own tactics. It should be remembered that while these tactics can be a stimulating mental challenge with very high financial rewards, they are not designed to provide a full-time source of income. They are designed to give the EG a little time and capital to survive and regroup to reenter the mainstream economy as a wiser person. These tactics, in various forms, have been successfully used and tested in the real world by many people. I know of no one who has had to resort to these strategies twice, and the majority of Economic Guerrillas have found themselves back on top within two years or less. It's completely up to you.

This section was not written for everyone. It was designed for an unfortunate and growing minority within our society, those who have to survive economic disaster. This calamity can strike anyone anywhere and the results can lead to unimaginable hardships. Many, many people are faced with the prospect of losing their homes, automobiles, friends, and family due to unforeseen economic reversals. The causes for this horror are varied, and can be as mundane as the "temporary layoff" or as complex as deadly "office politics." The effect is always the same. Those who have not experienced the absolute gut-twisting horror that comes from the collapse of an economic base cannot possibly understand the rage that is felt when the lack of funds seeps insidiously into every nook of daily life.

Few experiences can prepare one for the bone-rattling desperation that easily overtakes someone who is suddenly unemployed. For most people, being penniless and hungry at Christmas seems to be an abstract condition that we give passing lip service and maybe a couple of bucks to once a year. Not many of us take time to turn around and look into the eyes of the person in that position to see the rage, resentment, and defeat in that person's soul. It would make us too uncomfortable if we did.

The methods outlined in this section are not pretty or safely conventional. Poverty is not pleasant. These are tactics for *survival*. Some of the techniques will not fall into highly ethical or moral categories. Those who preach high ethics and moral standards are very seldom willing to underwrite someone's life with concrete action. These methods are last-ditch efforts before irreversible damage results from your economic depression. They are tough and dirty . . . they are also effective.

I will guarantee nothing, for these methods, or ones that you may develop on your own, will only work if you use them. A lyricist once wrote that the Wizard of Oz never gave anything to the Tin Man that he didn't already have. I sincerely hope you have the Economic Guerrilla instinct.

Debts

Millions of people begin each day with a debt load. For the majority, it represents a fair exchange for the lifestyle they enjoy. Others find debt a consuming whirlpool that sucks their creative talents continuously. These people have become unemployed or have lost their economic base. For them, debt is no longer a slight inconvenience. It is a rapidly growing monster. They experience a special type of hell with every mail delivery containing bills and registered letters. The stories they have heard concerning bill collectors, repossessions, and foreclosures take on a frightening reality. They take on a sense of desperation which is instantly communicated to potential employers or sources of income. These people may as well have a flashing neon sign on their foreheads . . . *loser*. This sets up a vicious circle. Debts cause desperation, desperation turns off employers, debts get bigger.

You are your creditor's best friend. Every time a business grants credit it is taking a gamble that it will get paid back with interest. The best assurance a business has of repayment is your morality. What about repossessions? The business usually loses more than it gains. The business has to pay for a court order, a process server, a moving van, and finally an auctioneer to resell the goods. Furniture and automobiles depreciate incredibly quickly once they leave the store. These goods depreciate even faster when they leave the home and travel to the auction barn. A business will usually net no more than 10 percent of the original value of the good, depending on the condition. Needless to say, a creditor is very reluctant to repossess in spite of threats to the contrary.

Foreclosures are the biggest headache a mortgage holder can have. If the average mortgage is paid out to the end of the amortization period, it will yield at least 300 percent of its face value. Not a bad return on an investment. If the bank has to foreclose, it stands to lose a great deal of money.

The mechanics of foreclosure are slow and cumbersome. They are also heavily weighted in favor of the homeowner. Laws vary in different areas, but in general a foreclosure goes something like this. The mortgage holder usually has to wait at least ninety days after the last payment is made before he can start any proceedings at all. At this point he has to start spending money on a lawyer to go to court. Even if you don't bother to show up in court, in some jurisdictions there's an automatic six-month period given for you to pay the amount owed.

This puts the mortgage holder on hold for at least another six months. If there is more than one mortgage holder, the latest one will try to get a court order, in some jurisdictions, to put the house up for sale. You can counteract this by listing the house yourself and doing nothing to encourage the sale. Keep the house messy, cook a lot of cabbage (the lingering aroma may discourage prospective buyers of the house), stop up the sinks, and don't cut the grass. What you are doing in reality is buying time to set up an alternative lifestyle somewhere else. You are converting the equity you have in your home into free rent for several months. You can also use the time to sell certain parts of the house, such as expensive chandeliers, carpeting, stained-glass windows, and other fixtures which you can replace with bare, minimum alternatives.

In fact, why not hold a massive garage sale? That's right, sell off absolutely everything that isn't essential. You are going to have to move anyway, so why not liquidate your noncritical assets now? You'll have a lot less stuff to move. Start looking now for accommodations that will be affordable in your present circumstances. You are not looking at the high-rent district. You are looking for something cheap. You aren't going to be there that long anyway. Try to avoid renting a house. They usually require that you pay full utilities on top of rent. Most apartments at least include hot water in the rent. When the final day comes and you have to leave your house, you have a secure base from which to operate. The mortgage holders have what's left of the house.

Credit-card companies fall into the category of unsecured creditors. They will usually scream the loudest if you don't pay them because they have no collateral to seize. Let them scream. They can't get blood from a stone. One Economic Guerrilla I knew stopped his mortgage and credit-card payments at the same time. The credit-card companies eventually placed liens against the house. At foreclosure time the mortgage holders and credit-card companies fought over what was left of the house and the guerrilla was long gone and set up elsewhere.

If you don't have a house, the unsecured creditors are in a worse position. After they have exhausted nasty little letters and collection agencies, they have to go to court to get a judgment. This costs them money in legal fees. The judgment states that you owe them money. You already knew that. They still have to collect it. If you have no income, they can't collect. If you are working and they find out where, then they can garnishee your wages, which usually puts you out of work, at which point they find themselves right back at square one.

Let's consider how the preceding information has affected your position. You have effectively let the courts relieve you of your debt load. It has not been without cost. Credit is a thing of the past and you will have to move to avoid being the target of collection agencies. There is another, much neater arrangement. Declare personal bankruptcy. This method either puts creditors on permanent hold or lets you repay them a greatly reduced amount on terms that are to your advantage. It is the only way to go if there is a family involved. Families do not have the mobility of a single person. Bankruptcy also allows you to keep the vast majority of your assets and remain employed. The net result is still the same, you don't have credit and you may have to move.

When you move, you should change a few things. Use a post office box for your mail. This will keep bill collectors off your doorstep. If you haven't already done so, clean out what's left of your bank account and put it in a safe-deposit box in another bank entirely. In yet another bank, set up a small account that will allow you to at least cash checks. Both of these will come in very handy later on. A telephone is a necessity. Make whatever peace you have to with the phone company, and get an unlisted number this time.

When you move, don't let the world know about it. Remember that the primary source of information concerning your whereabouts is you. The whole idea is to gain a little privacy and breathing space. You have now effectively gone "underground" with only Ma Bell and possibly a utility company knowing where you are. You have paid dearly for some time to breathe and regroup your energies. At this point, I want to introduce you to an old friend of mine, Mr. Murphy. Mr. Murphy has written laws which apply to all human beings:

Nothing is as easy as it looks.

Everything takes longer than expected.

If anything can go wrong, it will at the worst possible moment.

Ignore these laws at your own risk.

There's nothing like a good economic crisis to show what is really important and what is dead weight. Getting rid of dead weight is now a necessity. If you are looking for a good tool to use, go to the library and read a copy of Robert J. Ringer's *Looking Out for Number One*. Be prepared to be enlightened.

Welfare?

I would like to believe that it would be unnecessary to write this section. Unfortunately, that is naive. Some people describe the guerrilla philosophy as a massive cop-out. To those critics I say that if any one of them is prepared to completely underwrite the lives of any of the people who have been forced to use guerrilla tactics, I have seriously misjudged human nature. I wrote this manual for those who have the guts and dignity to reject the system of welfare which pays you to be alive. This manual is for those who have exhausted the so-called traditional means of meeting economic crisis and found the harsh reality that they are unemployable. It is my belief that giving these people a different tool is better than encouraging them to keep running up against a wall of frustration until they fall into the welfare pit.

The only person who benefits from the welfare system is the caseworker. Like a maggot, the caseworker thrives on waste and decay. He needs the misery of others to maintain good case-load statistics to justify his job. The last thing he wants to do is reduce his case-load statistics. His *primary* goal is to keep you dependent upon the government. When he can, through subtle manipulation, create second- and third-generation welfare families, it's a free bonus. To engage a social worker is to engage a maggot. Just consider what maggots eat and remember that they eat until there's *nothing* left.

Scavenging

Scavenging can be a very profitable endeavor for the EG. It consists of putting supply in touch with demand for a "small profit." The EG will utilize newspapers, swap meets, auctions, and garage sales as his tools.

Most larger communities have newspapers that specialize in advertising goods wanted and for sale by private individuals. These publications are as valuable to the EG as the *Wall Street Journal* is to the investor. They serve the same purpose. They let you know what is available, what is wanted, and what the going price is. In many cases, these papers advertise goods free of charge, so the EG has little overhead other than a telephone. To trade in this market you have to start out with inventory. The best place to get it is from your own home. Convert your noncritical assets into tax-free, working capital. You can either advertise one or two items by themselves or place an ad for a "garage sale" to move a large quantity of items. If possible, try to set aside in your safe-deposit box at least three hundred dollars from these sales -- you'll need this money later.

Once you have a little "working capital," you are ready to acquire (and definitely will need) more "inventory." Auction halls can be invaluable. I would advise anyone not familiar with auctions to spend a week or two traveling to various ones to see what types of merchandise auctions offer, what types of bids are made, and how items are bid upon and sold. I also advise carrying not more than five dollars with you at first to avoid impulse bidding. Try to sit near the rear of the hall, as this will allow you to see if the auctioneer is receiving real bids on items. Many a person has been tricked into bidding against himself because an auctioneer "appears" to be getting bids from a person just out of the bidder's range of vision. Keep an eye out for "spotters." These people are placed in a crowd to keep the bidding at a certain level. The easiest way of detecting spotters is to notice if the same people seem to "buy" a lot of items. Check to see if money actually changes hands at the end of the sale.

It would be unfair to say that all or even most auction halls use these practices. I would say maybe 3 percent at most. Remember, however, that you are spending your hard-earned money and you are the only one who is truly responsible for it, so don't immediately trust everyone who could possibly gyp it out of you.

You can turn your auction purchases into profits. You can reconsign them to the auction. This method allows you to let somebody else worry about selling it. Be prepared to pay the auctioneer a commission. You can advertise the product via newspapers. You can also market the product through garage sales and swap meets.

Swap meets are the closest thing to true "laissez-faire," free-enterprise capitalism toward which we in the United States strive. These meets represent the backbone of the scavenger trade. The combined weekly sales of swap meets across the United States have been estimated at over two hundred million dollars; this definitely is not small time. The swaps serve as a social gathering point for most local scavengers. It is not uncommon for these vendors to make two hundred to three hundred dollars a meet, while some make a lot more. This is usually clear money. No taxes, no licenses -- straight cash. Due to the large numbers of vendors involved, it is almost impossible for the authorities to regulate this type of underground economy.

To sell at the swap meets requires a bit of energy. As location is everything when participating in a swap meet, you should arrive very early in the morning to get the best spot in the hall. Bring a snack and proper clothing. Make sure you have an adequate cash float. Nobody, but nobody gives change. Fifty dollars in small bills and coin should be adequate. Also, don't go alone -- if you have to go to the washroom, or leave for any reason, you could easily be robbed blind by customers. Take a comfortable chair and possibly a radio. Keep your display attractive. Swap meets can be very entertaining -- and profitable once you have mastered the ground rules. You meet a variety of people and learn a great deal about human nature. You can make some very influential contacts with other vendors as well. The market is constantly growing and there is adequate room for anybody with the brains to make it work.

Firewood

I know it sounds crazy, but there is a lot of money to be made in firewood sales, especially if you live in a suburban or semi-rural area. Rising energy costs have resulted in phenomenal sales of wood-burning stoves and fireplace inserts. This means that there is an ever-increasing demand for good firewood. Most people would rather pay someone to deliver a few cords of wood than go out and cut it themselves. Why not let them pay you? Basically, you need a good chain saw, a sharp axe, a strong back, and a truck. Firewood doesn't always have to be derived from trees. Many woodworking plants have scraps that are free for the taking. Some such plants will even pay you to take it away for them. Demolition sites are also good sources of free wood.

When looking for a stand of timber, be sure to get the owner's permission to fell trees. New housing developments usually must have the land cleared before building can proceed. Often the timber is bulldozed and burned. You could probably get much of this scrap wood for free.

You'll need someplace to store your lumber once you've cut it. If you can't get free storage, try renting a backyard or garage from a friend. You'll want to cover the wood so that it can be reasonably dry by winter. Wood should usually dry for about six months.

One of the best places to advertise your services is at outlets that sell wood stoves and fireplaces. You can also put up signs in shopping centers and garden shops in your area. If all else fails, you may have to take out a small classified ad in your local paper.

Wood stoves are marvelous devices; they not only create a need for firewood, but for chimney sweeps as well. There simply aren't enough chimney sweeps to go around. If you don't mind getting a bit dirty, this can be a natural extension of your firewood business. How do you learn to be a chimney sweep? Excellent books are available at your library. Supplies are available at most hardware stores. To market yourself, simply drive around suburbia looking for stacked wood outside homes. Leave your flyer or card at the door if you're shy, it's even better to knock on the door and introduce yourself. Be prepared to be *very* busy.

Job Hunting

Not everyone has the inclination to handle the constant challenge of entrepreneurship. The security of a paycheck has many advantages. Obtaining a paycheck can be a lot easier if certain guerrilla tactics are used in the job search. The first tactic, of course, is modification of attitude.

Many job seekers think that employers are doing them a favor by hiring them. In fact, the opposite is true. To illustrate the point, let's go to the other side of the interview desk for a moment. When a position is vacant, the vacancy means that there is a breakdown in the company's efficiency caused by a missing body. This problem has to be fixed fast or the entire operation is in jeopardy. *Every* hiring officer has two major objectives: 1) to provide competent employees for the company (or get replaced himself), and 2) to get the most amount of productivity from an employee with the least amount of input, i.e., low training costs, high degree of skill, and manageable salary and benefit costs. If you fit the bill, you have done him a favor by providing your services.

Let's examine what you are actually doing when you job hunt. You are actually a salesman. You are selling the one thing that you are better qualified to sell than anyone else: yourself. You are selling yourself at a very expensive price. How expensive? Try a starting price of $432,000. That is what you would be paid if you started work at age twenty, for $5 per hour for a 160-hour month, and stayed at that salary until retirement at age sixty-five. That figure doesn't include benefits. In reality you will probably receive a lot more than $5 per hour during your working life, so you will be even more expensive. Now how hard are you going to work to sell your product?

The salesman who sells Rolls Royce motor cars knows he is selling a very expensive item to a select few while the Honda salesman is selling cheap to the masses. The Rolls Royce salesman won't drop the price of his product for a quick sale. He knows that if you have to hassle about the price, you don't deserve the product. The EG job hunter is in the same position as the Rolls Royce salesman in that he is selling quality goods at a high price.

The job hunter who knows his value has an immediate and decided advantage over every other job hunter. Most job hunters think they are selling Honda Civics -- secondhand ones at that. To the EG, a high unemployment rate simply means that the market is flooded with "cheap, used cars." A potential employer is like any other customer. He will buy the product that has the best presentation, the most attractive packaging, and the best quality for the price. You know that the customer can afford your product because he has "advertised" it. You also know the customer desires your product even if he doesn't know it yet. All you have to do is make the presentation and close the deal. Let's examine how that is done.

Any good salesman knows that he has to keep abreast of the competition and be responsive to market trends and customer needs. The same is true for the EG. When applying for a position, consider what the competition will be offering, i.e., dress, manner, skills, experience, and attitude. Use this information to put yourself ahead of the pack. Many job hunters think they will be judged for their ability and not their clothes. They are still looking for work. Poise and decorum have gotten more jobs than the new "laid-back" manner. Good manners go a long way because nobody uses them anymore. Respectful use of "yes ma'am/sir" is the rule in an interview, as is the gracious use of "please" and "thank you." When you go to an interview, you never know from where you are being observed, so be ready at least two blocks from the address. Don't smoke or have cigarettes visible, walk upright, look confident, make sure your hair is combed and cut, be clean and have trim nails. Know the name of the person you are going to see and be wary of the receptionist -- many otherwise successful interviews have been shot down because the personality the interviewee exhibited before the receptionist did not match the one shown in the interview.

Research the firm. Find out something about its products and its market. Get as much information as you can about its history. This will help you ask informed questions of the interviewer. The interviewer has probably seen a lot of people who are almost begging for jobs and have desperation oozing from their pores. If you enter appearing cool, confident, and competent, you have an incredible edge. The interviewer is not interested in whether or not you *need* a job or any of your personal problems. His only concern is what you can do for the company. Be prepared with at least five good reasons why you should be hired. Make sure they show the benefit to the company. If you are not asked, volunteer. Always have a resume. Nothing impresses an employer more than not having to go over the same old employment form. A resume gives you an opportunity to include much more information about yourself than possible in a job application form. Whether you mail in your resume or present it in person (preferred), *always* include a self-addressed and stamped envelope. This gets your resume back if you don't get the job, and in addition to saving photocopy costs, this makes the memory of you just a little stronger in the interviewer's mind, and it's just plain class.

If you wish to get your resume professionally prepared, look for a firm that uses a word processor. If your resume is stored on floppy disk, any revision or changes can be made very simply without having to retype the whole resume. When choosing a resume service, be sure to hire one that is willing to provide references. Talk to those references. If you can afford a professional resume service, this can be a very worthwhile investment.

When you have your interview, try to keep the interviewer talking. Ask him about the company. Base your questions on your research. What is the company's market share? What has been its annual growth percentage? Is that figure up to expectations? Where does the company see itself going in the next couple of years? How long has the interviewer been with the company? Does he feel comfortable with his rate of advancement? Would he mind showing you the facilities? The idea is to get the interviewer coming to you. You want the interviewer to try to "sell" you on the company.

At the close of the interview, get a firm commitment from the employer as to when you can expect to be informed of the results of the interview. Try to pin him down to a time of day that he will contact you. If you haven't heard from him by that time, contact him.

The most successful job-hunting technique I've found is the cold-turkey approach, an approach to a company that isn't hiring publicly. If you find a company that could use your skills, do your research, find who does the hiring, and present yourself. This is the most lucrative method of finding employment because the average employer realizes that it takes the most guts and only people who are truly committed to working will use it. Businessmen use the same technique to market their products, so the EG has the immediate empathy of the employers he approaches. Since there is no advertised vacancy, you usually aren't competing with anyone else, so you have a clear field and a little more time on your side.

Keep your ears open. If you take the bus, ask the

person next to you if he knows of any job openings. If you hitchhike, ask the person giving you a lift. Anywhere that people gather is a potential source of job leads, so exploit these resources. The unemployment rate is high, but people *are* getting hired every day and many of them are EGs selling Rolls Royces, so hang in there. If you must be a wage earner, remember that the Economic Guerrilla always plays with a stacked deck.

Aliases

The desire to just pack up and "disappear" when faced with financial crisis is very natural and very human. The idea of starting fresh in a new city with a new name and a new life can seem very attractive. I would strongly urge the EG not to take this route, however. Aliases have several inherent problems. Age, memory, verification, and family present the most difficulties.

The older one is, the harder it is to use an alias. A thirty-year-old male, for example, has not only to assume a new name, but thirty years of fictional, non-verifiable experiences as well. It is not as easy as it looks. An alias requires a good memory. You will be dealing with a wide variety of people, and you will have to be sure that every one of them receives the same consistent story. In many instances, it will become necessary to provide absolute proof-positive identification. This can be in the form of medical records, school transcripts, driver's licenses, passport applications, insurance regulations, or jobs that require a security clearance. This can be difficult if you are using an alias. If an EG is traveling with spouse and children, the problems multiply. The nonnuclear family can also create problems with an alias.

I have known EGs who have used aliases successfully. In the main, it required that they make a complete break with not only the past but with families as well. Some have started new families and feel some regret in knowing that their children may never know their true heritage. Others have no problem with this. Many have successfully rebuilt their lives, but the costs of the break have been high.

In some cases success itself can work against an EG using an alias. Many times success brings with it a certain degree of publicity. We live in an increasingly smaller world. It can be very uncomfortable for an EG when someone from his past life recognizes him from publicity.

If your circumstances are such that an alias is a viable alternative, be prepared to make sacrifices and commitments necessary for it to work. The EG should be very careful how he uses an alias. In general, an alias can be legally used if there is no intention to defraud. This is generally taken to mean that you must stay away from credit cards, but you're already doing this.

Many organizations sell new identification kits. They advertise driver's licenses, birth certificates, marriage licenses and other "official" documents. Every one of these documents is protected by law against forgery. In fact, some laws even prevent the photocopying of such documents. No business is going to openly advertise in national magazines and newspapers that they are breaking the law. What they will sell you is a less-than-useless piece of paper that could land you in jail depending on how you use it.

The information on how to get legitimate identification is readily available if you seek it out. Be very aware that you may be breaking the law and subject to imprisonment.

Home Security

The EG can profit from the home security market with a few simple tools and basic know-how. Door peepholes are very inexpensive and can be installed with just an electric drill and a screwdriver. Many people will be more than willing to pay seven to ten dollars per door for this service. It usually takes no more than five minutes per door. One of the easiest markets to access is apartment dwellers. An EG need only to place a flyer into each mailbox advertising the service. Many EGs have enlisted the help of the building manager to sell the whole building.

Locking night chains for doors and simple window locks can also be installed by the EG with simple tools such as a drill and screwdriver. Your local police department can be quite helpful in providing information concerning the best types to use. Inexpensive timers to turn lights on and off when the home is unoccupied are also very simple to install.

The enterprising EG can offer a "total package" of

inexpensive yet practical security items including all of the above. As a bonus, the EG can offer the use of an electric engraver to mark valuable items. It is best to offer to leave the engraver for twenty-four hours to allow the client privacy.

Sophisticated electronic alarms should be avoided for several reasons. These devices usually require that you have technical background to install properly. They are very expensive, can be difficult for nontechnical homeowners to operate and maintain, and can involve long-term after-sales service. Electronic alarm systems are also extremely sensitive to false alarms caused by poor installation, customer misuse, or equipment malfunction.

The simple home protection devices are usually available in most hardware stores. As the EG's business grows, he should be able to make larger purchases from hardware wholesalers at reduced prices.

Suggested Reading

Hill, Napoleon. *Think and Grow Rich Action Pack*, featuring *Think and Grow Rich*, by Napoleon Hill and the *Think and Grow Rich Action Manual*, 344 pages. New York: Hawthorne Books, 1972.

Jackson, Tom. *Guerrilla Tactics in the Job Market.* New York: Bantam Books, 1978.

Rand, Ayn. *Atlas Shrugged.* New York, Random House, 1957.

Rand, Ayn. *For the New Intellectual*, 192 pages. New York: Signet Books, The New American Library, 1961.

Rand, Ayn. *Capitalism: The Unknown Ideal*, 352 pages. New York: Signet, The New American Library, 1966.

Ringer, Robert J. *Looking Out for Number One*, 336 pages. Beverly Hills: Los Angeles Book Corp., 1977.

Ruff, Howard J. *How to Prosper During the Coming Bad Years*, a crash course in personal and financial survival, 256 pages. New York: Times Books, a division of Quadrangle/The New York Times Book Co., Inc., 1979.